# EXCUSES, EXCUSES!
## 100 REASONS WHY YOUR HORSE LOST THE RACE!

## JAMES A. VENA

Outskirts Press, Inc.
Denver, Colorado

This is a work of fiction. The events and characters described here are imaginary and are not intended to refer to specific places or living persons. The opinions expressed in this manuscript are solely the opinions of the author and do not represent the opinions or thoughts of the publisher. The author represents and warrants that s/he either owns or has the legal right to publish all material in this book.

Excuses, Excuses
100 Reasons Why Your Horse lost the Race!
All Rights Reserved
Copyright © 2006 James A. Vena

Cover Image © 2006 JupiterImages Corporation
All Rights Reserved. Used With Permission.

This book may not be reproduced, transmitted, or stored in whole or in part by any means, including graphic, electronic, or mechanical without the express written consent of the publisher except in the case of brief quotations embodied in critical articles and reviews.

Outskirts Press
http://www.outskirtspress.com

ISBN-10: 1-59800-592-8
ISBN-13: 978-1-59800-592-9

Library of Congress Control Number: 2006927900

Outskirts Press and the "OP" logo are trademarks belonging to
Outskirts Press, Inc.

Printed in the United States of America

# PREFACE

There is an old adage that trainers of racehorses use when a new owner applies for an owner's license for the first time. "Owners trade in their brains for an owner's license when they enroll as new horse owners."

I have heard this a great many times while I witnessed all the trainers circling the wagons of the new owner as if it was a fresh kill, when the license is approved.

You see, the sport of kings as it is called is truly the greatest sport in the world. The reason I know this is because I was caught up in it for many years and truly felt like a king while the times were good. The king's ransom that it costs an owner in tuition alone is relatively innocuous for the first part of most owners' experiences. It's only felt years later when the thrill is gone and you realize that you really did leave your brains behind when they handed you your license to own and buy your treasured racehorses.

Aside from being at the Belmont Stakes watching Secretariat win the Triple Crown, I really can't recall ever being caught up in the world of thoroughbreds.

I was 13 at the time and spent many Saturdays at the racetrack with my father, who loved the ponies. My dad liked betting on horses and going to the races more than anyone I ever knew. Frankly I never really understood why anyone would like to lose money more often than not while being in a smoke-filled setting, spending most of the day standing in line, eating lousy food, and ripping up tickets. He did love it, though, and it really was part of his life and enjoyment.

So somewhere around my 35th birthday, I decided that it would be fun to buy a horse and re-develop a bond with my dad. We could have something to do together, which would be a nice way to spend the mornings and some afternoons. Since I moved out of the family house to get married and start my own family, the years went by so quickly that I really wanted to get a horse for us to share. So I did just that…

Well, this horse racing business has a way of getting into your blood (and wallet). No, not the gambling side of the business; you don't need to own racehorses to bet on them. Rather, the emotional side of the business is what gets new owners hooked. The business in general as well as the horses become part of your identity. You become hooked like a junkie on dope in this very seductive and exciting industry. Trainers along with backstretch personnel know this and seize the opportunity to take their piece of you before there is nothing left of you but the memories.

Through the years of watching my horses run, I found the reasons (excuses) an owner would hear when their horse just lost a race comical and well-constructed.

In the beginning, the reasons (excuses) all sounded logical. However, after time, and after one puts their brains back into place, the reasons (excuses) become more and more repetitive. Finally I realized that the majority of these reasons were nothing more than excuses. I often kidded with my trainers that I was going to number these excuses so that they can just tell me the corresponding number. I would be able to then just go to the menu and see what I will tell all those I know, why I keep investing in this loser! All of this while the trainer is trying to encourage me not to give up on this horse just yet. Thus the excuses!

Well, I am now out of the racing business, perhaps not forever. My father has taken up golf and hung up his racetrack spikes. The man who loved the races found out that the horses were better than many of the people that are around them, ruining his love of the sport altogether.

I have very fond memories of the racing business and miss it from time to time. In the meantime I have written this list of 100 excuses, with real stories that pertain to each excuse as I recall hearing them. I hope you enjoy them and end up using them like a guide to indicate to your trainer or jockey that you are on to them.

*I dedicate this book to my Family*

First and foremost to my wife Debbie, who was as excited for me during the good times in the winner's circle, as she was supportive of me when things weren't so rosy. Funny thing is that she now enjoys horses about as much as I did. She, however, will keep her horse affinity toward breeding stock and show horses!

My son James and daughter Jacqueline are both my life's blood, and while James only has fond memories of our travels in the world of thoroughbred racing, he no longer has any interest in them. Thankfully, James now focuses his attention on his education, baseball, and his upcoming foray into the business world. Jacqueline has truly become the real horse aficionado in our family. Because of all this, Jacqueline has been around horses from a very young age. Her pony Misty is very lucky to have Jacqueline as her rider and owner. Jacqueline will hopefully continue toward a career with horses as they seem to be her passion. Since I already paid a large tuition, I hope to share it with her someday. It can be the bond that all fathers dream about having with their daughters.

Of course, none of this would have been possible without my Mom and Dad. Joan and "Sonny" were great throughout this era of my life. They were both there for all the great horse racing memories (there were a bunch). Their parenting is what makes me who I am.

A very special thank you to my friend Stuart Held, who helped me immensely in putting this book together and truly inspired me to take a crack at writing my first book.

# TABLE OF CONTENTS

Excuse # 1:"Needed the race"
Excuse # 2 :"Flipped his palate"
Excuse # 3 :"Didn't like dirt in his face"
Excuse # 4 :"Got left at the gate"
Excuse # 5 :"Hung"
Excuse # 6:"Spun his wheels"
Excuse # 7:"Needs blinkers on"
Excuse # 8:"Needs blinkers off"
Excuse # 9:"Horse ran green"
Excuse #10:"Got bumped"
Excuse #11:"Jock didn't let him run"
Excuse #12:"Needs Lasix"
Excuse #13:"Too much Lasix"
Excuse #14:"Stood too long in gate"
Excuse #15:"Jock fell asleep"
Excuse #16:"Horse has no heart"
Excuse #17:"Didn't fit the rider"
Excuse #18:"Left race in his last work"
Excuse #19:"Needs a tongue tie"
Excuse #20:"Doesn't like the tongue tie"
Excuse #21:"Race came up too tough"
Excuse #22:"Needs to be gelded"
Excuse #23:"Horsing in Post Parade"

Excuse #24: "Rider asked him too early"
Excuse #25: "Rider asked him too late"
Excuse #26: "Race was too long"
Excuse #27: "Race was too short"
Excuse #28: "Hated the inside post"
Excuse #29: "Hated the outside post"
Excuse #30: "Hated horses on both sides"
Excuse #31: "Horse needs grass"
Excuse #32: "Track was cuppy"
Excuse #33: "Track was too hard"
Excuse #34: "Likes the mud"
Excuse #35: "Hated the mud"
Excuse #36: "Horse got out"
Excuse #37: "Horse lugged in"
Excuse #38: "Bad karma in the barn"
Excuse #39: "Rider lost the whip"
Excuse #40: "Lost a shoe"
Excuse #41: "Ran down"
Excuse #42: "Grabbed his quarter"
Excuse #43: "Was hot nailed in the A.M."
Excuse #44: "Needs caulks"
Excuse #45: "Didn't like the caulks"
Excuse #46: "Rider stopped whipping"
Excuse #47: "Horse hated being hit"
Excuse #48: "Horse was short"
Excuse #49: "Lost stirrup"
Excuse #50: "Bled"
Excuse #51: "Saddle was too loose"
Excuse #52: "Saddle was too tight"
Excuse #53: "Teeth need to be done"
Excuse #54: "Feet need to be done"
Excuse #55: "Jumped a shadow"
Excuse #56: "Doesn't like the heat"
Excuse #57: "Hates the cold"
Excuse #58: "Doesn't like racing under lights/heat index/day of the week/stage of the moon, etc."

Excuse #59: "Got spooked by crowd"
Excuse #60: "Needs to relax"
Excuse #61: "Ankles are bugging him"
Excuse #62: "Knees are bugging him"
Excuse #63: "Shins are bugging him"
Excuse #64: "Feet are bugging him"
Excuse #65: "Just not right today"
Excuse #66: "Washed out in the gate"
Excuse #67: "Didn't sweat at all"
Excuse #68: "Needs wraps"
Excuse #69: "Didn't like the wraps"
Excuse #70: "Hated the color of wraps"
Excuse #71: "Ran into a brick wall"
Excuse #72: "Can't handle the mental pressure of being a racehorse"
Excuse #73: "Too intelligent"
Excuse #74: "Too loopy"
Excuse #75: "Can't run with these"
Excuse #76: "Speed was holding"
Excuse #77: "Speed wasn't holding"
Excuse #78: "Hates to be rushed"
Excuse #79: "Hates to be restrained"
Excuse #80: "Hates to pass horses"
Excuse #81: "Hates the new bit"
Excuse #82: "Ran out of room"
Excuse #83: "Ran out of racetrack"
Excuse #84: "Ran out of trainer at the 1/16th pole"
Excuse #85: "Needs wider turns"
Excuse #86: "Ran as far as he could"
Excuse #87: "Ran as fast as he could"
Excuse #88: "Needs some time off"
Excuse #89: "Needs to be run right back"
Excuse #90: "Needs a new environment"
Excuse #91: "Needs a Bug rider"
Excuse #92: "Needs an experienced rider"
Excuse #93: "Needs a rider with a better left hand"
Excuse #94: "Needs a rider with a better right hand"

Excuse #95:"Needs better handed rider"
Excuse #96:"Stepped on a stone"
Excuse #97:"Stepped in a hole"
Excuse #98:"Can't keep up with these"
Excuse #99:"Not bred to run young"
Excuse #100:"Not bred to be here"

# EXCUSE 1
## "NEEDED THE RACE"

My jockey was talking to the trainer—confidentially—however, loud enough for me and the "new" owner entourage to be able to overhear the excuse. It sounded perfectly reasonable. The horse was coming off a layoff of 17 days, and the jockey thought the encouraging words of "needing the race" would soothe my ego as an owner.

I jumped to the conclusion that the jockey was telling us the next time out we would be in the winner's circle. The horse needed a couple of minutes to work out the kinks, and that seemed to have been accomplished—today!

The jockey actually told the trainer, in a stage voice, "Make sure I get to ride this horse next time; he is sitting on a win." I was excited – we were going to soon be in the winner's circle. After what I heard from the jockey, I never looked at the facts. The horse has been in training under the best of trainers available for $85 per day. Why would I care if the horse needed to race rather than train? I was going to end up in the winner's circle next week.

The next race—a week later—the trainer dropped the horse in for a claiming tag. The rider who I thought was making a date in the winner's circle with me had a previous commitment to ride another horse in the same race. Wow, I thought, what a guy—he would rather lose a race to keep his previous commitment to another owner to ride his horse. This is loyalty!

We ended up with a "bug boy," for this race and the horse finished somewhere up the track. After all, everyone knew that it was a clear sign that the race the horse needed was to prove that we didn't give him enough time to heal his injury. Well, almost everyone knew—I didn't. Owners are always the last to know!

I thought we were in for a win, so I invited family members and friends to come take a picture of us in the winner's circle. However, to this day I wonder how the jockey knew that he would still be in the winner's circle that day. Needless to say he won the race on the mount he had "previously'" organized.

# EXCUSE 2
## "FLIPPED HIS PALATE"

There we were, all dressed up and waiting for the race to be over with so we could take our win picture, cash our winning tickets, and call our friends and associates who couldn't make it to the track that day, just to rub it in that we were having a great time ,while they were still at the office.

Well, at least we thought that this was the scenario that was going to take place. I mean, the horse was out in front by seven or eight lengths as they approached the 1/8th pole. Who would have thought that with only another 10 or 12 seconds left until this was a race ready for the books that it could end so badly? We were going to winner's circle, right?

Wrong! Without warning, the horse stopped as the others came on like a cavalry charge and passed him. We were witnessing our horse appear to go backwards. Suddenly, like sinking in quicksand, the racing gods let the horse beat one out of his nine foes. Dazed and confused, I was standing there waiting for the horse to come back so I could listen and hear what had caused such a letdown. The rider came off and the trainer asked, "Did he have a problem breathing?" The rider responded that the horse was making a funny noise as he turned for home and suggested that we have the horse "scoped." The vet came to the barn and stuck a long rubber tube into the horse's nostril and proclaimed, "He flipped his palate!"

I immediately wondered what the horse was doing with a palate! I am told that it is a slang term for a horse that had an epiglottis displacement. The horse couldn't get his air intake, so he couldn't continue to race hard!

Still dazed and confused, I asked what could have caused such a problem. I was told that the horse was so excited to win that his nervousness caused this displacement. An equipment change should cure this, I was told. Reaching into my pocket to get the 60 bucks to pay this vet for seeing what the jockey heard for free, I came across my win and place tickets along with my cell phone, which showed seven missed calls.

I ripped up all of the tickets, paid the vet, and retrieved my phone messages. Yes, they were from the same people I was thinking of calling only an hour ago to taunt about not being able to come join me in the winner's circle on this glorious day. Now I have to call them all back only to explain that everything is just dandy with my horse with the exception of the "flipping of the palate" story. They will be less gullible than I when I tell them I ripped up their tickets, too!

# EXCUSE 3
## "DIDN'T LIKE DIRT IN HIS FACE"

Can you imagine that the horse didn't enjoy get dirt sprayed in his face from all of the horses that were in front of him? As they were going around the track, he wasn't happy at all at eating dust as they call it in the cowboy movies. He wasn't fast enough to keep up, so he just got pummeled with sand and stone in his face. The trainer, of course, jumped at the opportunity to let me know not to give up on him as we still have hope that he will like the turf, so the dirt won't be a problem. I guess some horses that are just born slow would prefer to get hit with clumps of grass divots rather than dirt and sand. To each his own, I suppose, but personally I would still rather be paying this $85 a day on a faster horse that was kicking up the dirt and dust to all of those looking at his hindquarters. When it comes to kicking up sand, dirt, and dust, I think it truly is better to give than to be on the receiving end!

# EXCUSE 4
## "GOT LEFT AT THE GATE"

All of this time in training, I noticed that there is a lot of extra attention spent on getting the horse to go in and out of the gate smoothly. This is so important that a special certificate is given to a racehorse when they are ready to break from the gate like a racehorse. It's like a diploma, allowing the student to move on to the really important stuff that is in front of him. All of this training and a little tipping to the gate crew for their hard efforts will now pay off with a trip to the winner's circle, I am told, and we are a slam dunk to hit the board in the first start as we are working really well in the morning! We all get ready to witness this horses coming of age to gain respectability, not to mention to earn some purse money to pay this ever increasing pile of training bills. We are all very excited and oozing with anticipation.

The gate opened up, and my horse was so confident that he was better trained than all of the others that he spotted the field six lengths in the first few seconds of the race. Well, we did pass a couple of horses before the race was over, so at least there was some good news. One could argue the horses we did pass were tired (I thought perhaps they all flipped their palates), but we seem to have a closing type of horse anyway. We did get a lot of experience for the next race.

The jockey was excited about passing the tired horses, too! That's when I was informed that if we didn't get "left in the gate" we would have won by a quarter poles. Unless, of course, he would have flipped his palate from the excitement of getting out of the gate too quickly! You see, I really am learning!

# EXCUSE 5
## "HUNG"

So there you are, watching your horse go from last in the pack to third, passing horses one at a time as they approach the final turn of the race. Full of excitement and anticipation, you are thinking to yourself, this time "the gate break was good," he is not on too big a lead, so chances are he will not get "too excited" and "spit the bit," or "flip his palate." Hmmm. Maybe, just maybe, today is the day! Suddenly you note that he is maneuvering around the dirt, and more importantly, the dirt that's hitting him in the face isn't really bothering him. So what could go wrong now, you wonder.

Well, he just doesn't seem to be able to catch up to the winner and runner-up. He finishes a well-beaten third. Finally at least we get paid for our good gate break and keeping our palate in place, but it sure would be nice to finish first and get the big part of the pot while taking that elusive picture in the winner's circle!

The rider hops off and says we "hung." What does that mean? Surely we can "un-hang" him in the next race, right? Maybe some equipment change will help. So what does hung mean anyway?

It means that your horse is no longer gaining on the competition! I think to myself (as I try to believe this excuse), will they be slower next time? I hope so! Then I immediately get an idea of renaming this horse "Cheap Suit."

# EXCUSE 6
## "SPUN HIS WHEELS"

The gate opens and we break well; we don't need the race this time. We are not on the lead where now I worry about flipping a palate! We are just running sort of evenly with the pack. I thought to myself, this rider is doing a real good job of rating this horse, while keeping him interested in the race. Not pushing too fast or asking him for more too early.

Well, thank the stars above that this race was a short sprint! The race that we were never in contention only lasted a minute and 12 seconds. That's long enough to suffer! The horse never even got a mention from the track announcer. Rider tells us after dismounting that we can run with these, but he just "spun his wheels" out there today!

Frankly I still don't really know what that meant. I have had a lot of horses run this lethargically, so there must be something to this losing of races because of traction! Maybe I should have renamed one "Bald Tire."

# EXCUSE 7
## "NEEDS BLINKERS ON"

This seems like a logical reason (excuse) to tell all of your friends and loved ones that told you not to throw your money away on racehorses in the first place.. The trainer and jockey make a compelling argument that the horse will run faster and longer if only he had paid attention to the race and not the traffic or the crowd. Maybe he was looking at the lake on the infield with the pretty trees and shrubbery. So we "don the shades" as they say. This is trainer speak for putting the "blinkers on."

Well, with the shades on, the horse busts out of the gate like a flash! He is not spinning his wheels this time. He is now running like the wind. All of a sudden the reality sets in that the blinkers may have made him run a little faster early on, but those shades didn't give the horse any additional stamina! At least we got several calls from the track announcer today; the most notable was when he said our horse "checked out of the race and had nothing left."

# EXCUSE 8
## "TAKE THE BLINKERS OFF"

After your horse performs as ours did with the blinkers on, you can bet your money that the rider will tell you to take the blinkers off for the next race. He'll tell you that your horse is now learning how to run and win on his own. Boy, those horses are really smart! Self educated no less!

I remember once winning with the blinkers on, and as the track announcer declared us "saved by the wire," I suddenly started wondering what excuse the owner of the horse that finished third was being told. I think that horse may have flipped his palate! The glass being half full theory tells me his trainer told him that our horse was saved by the "flipped palate" of his horse and not the finish line!

# EXCUSE 9
## "HORSE RAN GREEN"

Watching my horse run and covering every inch of the track as if he were running a zigzag pattern on an Easter egg hunt was a little unsettling. The trainer was telling me how "green" the horse was running as they were on the backside. He also informed me that this was to be expected in the horse's first start. Boy, those horses really are smart!

I guess from time to time the horses make sure that the trainer doesn't get too much credit! Today he was showing us that all of the time and money invested in training him really wasn't necessary at all. After all, according to my trainer, he was going to need the race anyway. Hey, where have I heard that before!

Well, after the race was over I was as green as the horse that just ran. My green tint, though, was green with envy as the other first time starter was getting his picture taken in the winner's circle with his proud owner! He must have had the smarter horse, I suppose!

# EXCUSE 10
## "GOT BUMPED"

When you are just a spectator or a casual better at the track, you tend to not care enough about the race that just finished to actually watch the race replays from the head-on view.

However, when you graduate to being an astute owner and student of the game and own a horse that just lost a race, the 10 minutes or so that follow the race are usually spent watching the various race replays. Different camera angles and different speeds are shown on all of the track's televisions so that one can either Monday morning quarterback, celebrate, or come up with a reason (excuse) of why the horse didn't win the race. It's like therapy! It takes your mind off of the agony of defeat and the reality that no purse money is coming again, while you and the trainer commiserate to discuss all the "what ifs."

The first time I heard that we "got bumped" I frankly didn't see it while the race was being run. I was watching as intently as the others, and I don't think they saw the "bump" either, despite what they said afterward. Well, the rider comes back and says that we were in good position and just about ready to make our winning move when the inside horse made contact with us.

Let's go to the videotape! The rider was right! Coming out of the gate, we were slammed! You couldn't see it on the pan view, but the head-on shot clearly showed the injustice!

Now what? Well, nothing really. It was just another day at the races. You see, if you watch every race from the head-on view, you'd be as surprised as I was when you see the contact that goes on as horses and their riders jockey for position. It's more of an oddity when horses don't bump.

On that day, this novice owner learned a whole lot more about the game now that I was a proud student. Excuses, excuses. The fastest horse won the race, so stop your crying!

# EXCUSE 11
## "JOCK DIDN'T LET HIM RUN"

Well, why wouldn't the rider (jock) let the horse run, you may ask yourself. After all, they only get paid the real money when they win. So why is the trainer and staff telling me that the jock "ain't letting him run" while he is trailing the field by some 15 lengths as they turn for home?

I am totally embarrassed that I asked a few friends to come out and watch my horse run today.

However, I guess I now have an excuse of why he is getting pummeled and looking like he doesn't belong in races with other thoroughbreds. It's the rider's fault! The "jock" is not letting him run.

I am thinking that perhaps next time the jock "lets him run" at even higher odds than the 55-1 that we are at today, we can't lose. They must be looking to get a better price next week when we will all be bursting with the glee, having bet the 75 or 80 to one shot that the jock is going to "let run" and make up those 35 lengths we just got beat by today!

Well, that's only for the movies! "He doesn't really love me" when it comes to gambling like that guy in the movies. Truthfully, the rider (jock) was doing the best he could on what he had underneath him. Unfortunately, sometimes horses just are not sound enough to allow the rider to "let them run." Have no fear, though, my trainer has the answer! A bug boy (apprentice) for the next race! They always try hard and will risk life and limb to prove that they belong even if the horse doesn't.

# EXCUSE 12
## "NEEDS LASIX"

They all need Lasix, I thought! If that's what the others are running on, then why shouldn't we? Why weren't we on the stuff in the first place! What is the percentage of horses that win without the product nowadays anyway? Let's play the percentages, or shall I dare say the odds, as that's a better way of putting it in this business.

Lasix is a brand name of a diuretic. It supposedly helps horses run faster by treating them all as bleeders. I once read that the long-term effect is debilitating, which is why I guess it works and everyone uses it. Like steroids, I suppose. "No pain, no gain."

I used to have a very humane, holier than thou attitude, when it came to animals, and would actually prefer that they just ban the stuff for the sake of the horses. However, as the bills start mounting and the winner's circle is getting so elusive, we all quietly tuck our feelings and humane side away for the sake of prosperity. When told that we should try it, I couldn't help wondering silently why we would even compete without it in the first place. The excuse worked, though, as it gave us hope that the next time would be the time for us to take a win picture! My horse would finally be on an even playing field with the others in the race. Okay, so this horse may be the

"Bees Knees," to us, but he is not loaded with so much talent that we can give an edge to the others and still win. I should have renamed this one "Sell Out." I did in fact sell out my animal humane beliefs for a chance to take a picture and get the much needed purse money.

# EXCUSE 13
## "TOO MUCH LASIX"

Funny how I didn't notice that the horse, now on Lasix for the first time, wasn't acting any different in the saddling area or post parade. We'll come back to that later!

So the race program has a big fat "FTL" next to my horse's name, meaning FIRST TIME LASIX. The stuff is important enough that not only is the dosage governed by the racing officials, but the bettors must be made aware of who is on, or more aptly, not on the super juice. There is a whole contingency of handicappers out there that use this not so inside information in selecting their wagering choices. (And we ran without the stuff last time!!!) Now with Lasix in tow, we race against the same field that trounced us last time, sans the winner who went on to bigger and better races. Well, we got thoroughly trounced again. This time, however, I was really miffed. I mean, we had the dose of Lasix, so can it be that we just are out of reasons and have to face the fact that this guy was money not so well spent? Could it be he just wasn't good enough to run against these? Well, just as I am thinking that it would be a lot easier on the horse and my wallet to 'fess up to the fact that he needs to be at a lesser track with lesser purses and lesser training bills, I am now being encouraged that this marvel of a racehorse is just fine!! The problem the rider and trainer speculated was that the dose of Lasix was too much for him! He was so relaxed that he got lethargic. They both were talking to each other about how quiet he was in the saddling area. Almost asleep on his feet, they say. I was impressed that the rider remembered the horse from three weeks ago enough to critique his behavior while in the saddling area. Well, maybe next time we will get the dosage just right!

# EXCUSE 14
## "STOOD TOO LONG IN THE GATE"

Yes, there are times when the race has a fractious horse that just will not go into the starting gate with the style and ease of the rest of the field. While the gate crew is manhandling the horse that has decided to be stubborn today, all of the horses that were previously loaded have to stand there awaiting this ill-behaved monster to load. While all of this sounds innocent enough, the horses that lose have the excuse that it was the waiting and standing in the gate too long that cost them the race. They expelled too much energy just waiting. Except, of course, for the winner; he must have had some gate waiting in his bloodlines or maybe even was trained to be gentleman like while awaiting the others to load.

I thought there may be a sliver of truth to this. Then again when you lose, hope is all you can go on, and being the eternal optimist, I figured such a disaster couldn't happen twice, so we'd be okay with this guy next time. I kept telling myself that as I paid the next training bill!

# EXCUSE 15
## "JOCK FELL ASLEEP"

I guess he just didn't see that fast horse coming at him and ultimately pass him in the stretch! Maybe the rider wore the blinkers today! If only he would have been awake; he would have hit the turbo-charge button so the tiring horse he was on would have propelled to the finish line first. I wonder if the winner was told how lucky he was that my guy fell asleep at the turbo switch. Well, we all get tired, even the horses.

# EXCUSE 16
## "HORSE HAS NO HEART"

Well, he had one when we bought him! As a matter of fact, for the last two years he was in training he must have had one for us to all be here hoping to win today! I couldn't have been investing all of this time and money in an animal that was born without a heart. Where did we buy him from? Oz?

So where did the heart go if it's not there anymore? Do we get a refund for buying such a handicapped animal? I wondered why we bothered to look at the pedigree and confirmation when we didn't even make sure that he had something to pump his blood.

Next time my horse is racing and the bigger, stronger, and faster horses run right by him, I'll shout to the rider, "Excuse # 16!" and hopefully he would have memorized this excuse in the manual and understand that the reason the horse slowed down is because he may be looking for his heart!

# EXCUSE 17
## "DIDN'T FIT THE RIDER"

When I first heard this excuse, I had to wonder what the rider didn't have to not fit the horse. Now I know the truth. This rider wanted to be on a horse that can win a race!

Why is it that I always end up with the speed rider on my slow horses and a patient plodder on my really quick ones? Hmmm…we better do a more thorough job in finding a rider who understands the real needs of this diamond in the rough!

# EXCUSE 18
## "LEFT RACE IN HIS LAST WORK"

Well, the excitement one feels when getting the phone call from the trainer advising that your horse was the fastest of all horses breezing this morning is indescribable. Sort of like that feeling you get when you know you had the right answers for an upcoming test when you were in school. The cat who ate the canary is the look that you are trying to conceal as you hang up the phone and eagerly tell your cronies about the good times that will be had by all in six days or so, when the race comes up in the condition book. You clear your calendar and make certain that you can be at the races that day.

Well, look at this! The racing office was foolish enough to write a race three days from now for some hotshot, well-connected trainer or owner and actually called my trainer to ask us to run in that race. I am thinking this must be my lucky week, and that's the reason why the racing gods want us to race this week and not next week.

After the horse gets waxed by the horse that they wrote the race for, I hear the rider tell the trainer that the horse was so good and sharp in the Tuesday morning workout that he probably left his race on the training track that morning. There have been so many times this excuse has been used, that they named a breed of horse after the excuse. They refer to this type of horse as a "morning glory!" I had lots of "morning glories"
.

# EXCUSE 19
## "NEEDS A TONGUE TIE"

A tongue tie is a strip usually made of leather, cloth, or latex and is tied over the horses tongue in a race in order to prevent the tongue from getting over the bit and being yanked or pulled back into the horse's throat. A tongue tie is not a novel idea, just a good sound one. Sort of like tying your shoelaces before going out for a morning jog.

So my horse stops as if he was shot by a sharpshooter in the clubhouse, and nearly suffocates himself and collapses as he chokes on his own tongue. Cleverly the rider would never tell the trainer that the horse needs a tongue tie (because they all do) but says that the tongue tie that the trainer or groom obviously forgot, or didn't put on right, would have made a huge difference in the race. Sounds good to me! I never actually tried to perform or compete at anything while choking on my own tongue, but it sure can't be easy! To think we only lost by a couple of lengths while given such a handicap. Victory will surely be had next time. Let's write another check!

# EXCUSE 20
## "DOESN'T LIKE THE TONGUE TIE"

As incredible as it sounds (I swear to you), I have actually heard this more times than you could possibly imagine. The horse supposedly played with the tongue tie and was trying to get it off, which is why he wasn't paying enough attention in order to win today. Choking on his tongue will certainly get his attention next time, and then he'll win, right? You might as well tie those laces on your shoes together and see how far you can run.

# EXCUSE 21
## "RACE CAME UP TOO TOUGH"

To think that before the race they were all Maidens!

I guess we weren't really supposed to be finishing in front of that horse that cost three million dollars at a public auction. I mean, there must be some benefit to spending that sort of money for a horse aside from the fact that he could win a beauty contest. Perhaps we should have waited for all these high-priced horses to break their maiden, or better yet, run at a racetrack that is beneath these types of horses. Those low purses aren't good enough for them. Well, the trainer said we belonged in Saratoga. I am getting the feeling that this horse paid his ticket to an all-expense-paid vacation that I gladly paid in the name of horses, hopes, and dreams.

I must admit, however, that before we went into the starting gate, I wasn't thinking any of these negative and cynical thoughts. I thought that we did belong because the trainer told me so before we paid all of these extraneous expenses. I was deceived! No, it can't be. He must be right. This was just an extra tough field.

# EXCUSE 22
## "NEEDS TO BE GELDED"

Gelding a horse! The ultimate equipment change!

Let's help this guy keep his mind on the races by removing his testicles is what I am told. This preposterous idea is a typical knee-jerk reaction to a horse that is a handful in the barn. I am told that they don't need those testicles since most won't be going to the stallion barn anyway. I am glad, as you should be, that we are not racehorse's! I would prefer to keep mine long after my breeding days are over!

The problem here is that it is really impossible to confirm that this method of such a drastic makeover really does work. Trainers have told me that many great horses were better off after they were castrated and became geldings. Then again, many horses get better for no apparent reason as they mature and get older. What is really the difference to needing a race? Perhaps we could have let him keep his coveted family jewels if we were a little more cautious with the steroids, hormones, and the rest of the chemical concoctions we used to make him more aggressive.

Gelding a horse is just another option that trainers can use to keep the horse in the barn while the owner is hanging on hope that this will be the equipment change necessary to compete with these! I always wondered why they had to designate whether a horse is a gelding or not in the race program. Makes you wonder why they need to let everyone know about your horse's loss of manhood.

# EXCUSE 23
## "HORSING IN THE POST PARADE"

Sort of like a colt that is studdish in the post parade, a filly will be accused of horsing when she is looking around and feeling amorous while in the paddock or post parade. With all of the hormones she was given, we now have a filly that wants to be a mare or, even worse, a stud colt!

Like the horse that needs to take the blinkers off, or the horse that needs a race, this filly ran like she was ripping and ready to get to the finish line first, but ran out of gas.

Well, this girl of mine is in her fourth race. After putting on the tongue tie, jacking her up with Lasix, and taking the blinkers off, we had the same outcome as the other three races. Have no fear, though, because instead of finishing eighth, we finished fourth. Vast improvement and some purse money to boot. I am not at all paying close enough attention that the reason we keep getting closer is most likely due to the fact that the winners are moving on to better quality races. The second and third place finishers of those previous races are now finishing first and second. We are bound to win by attrition!!!

However sensible and logical the thought of winning by attrition may be, trainers have to train and bill for such services. They had me believing that all of the changes were getting us closer. And today we would have beaten the odds and won if not for the rider telling us that she was horsing today and just a drop of this and a dab of that will make the next race the winning race! Then I am informed that this horsing filly was very studdish in behavior during the cueing up toward the gate. Quickly thinking of the steroids she has been on to bulk her up, it dawns on me that I should change her name to "Lola."

# EXCUSE 24
## "RIDER ASKED HIM TOO EARLY"

    Showing up at the races with racing form in hand, you will see friends and colleagues that all have the perfect racing strategy to get your horse to the winner's circle.
    Breaking from a particular post on this particular day, against this particular field, means that to win we need to be in the front, so they tell me. The trainer tells the rider, while giving the pre-race instructions, to break sharply from the gate, go to the front and improve the horse's position. So the horse rolls out of the starting gate, and the rider makes the lead quite easily. As the horse is opening up on the field, by a few lengths, then six lengths, nine lengths, etc, you note that at this pace you will be breaking the track record. The rider is whipping and driving to keep him on a comfortable 12-length lead when they turn for home. The lead is now dwindling 10 lengths, eight lengths, three lengths, and you pray the finish line is coming soon. The rest of the field now passes your horse, which is on its hands and knees just to finish the race, and you cross the line dead last. The trainer now tells you that your horse went too fast too soon. To think I thought only a few minutes ago about the newspaper clipping for the scrapbook about my horse owning a track record. I guess the seven pounds we were getting off with this apprentice rider just wasn't enough to make up for his pedal to the metal style.

# EXCUSE 25
## "RIDER ASKED HIM TOO LATE"

Well, after the last performance, it was decided by the trainer to make a rider change as the apprentice rider (bug boy) just didn't know how to rate a horse. With the blinkers on and all the speed, the experienced but heavier rider would have a better chance to sit and rate this guy who has now been sitting on a win for three months if not for a bunch of bad luck. Rather than training him differently with perhaps some long stamina-building gallops, we blamed the rider for not being able to harness and throttle down that early, cheap speed.

The journeyman rider climbs aboard, and the trainer tells him to take back and make one run with him in the stretch.

Perhaps it was the quarter-mile breezes, or the new feed and medication, but this horse was looking like a horse that meant business today. Like a tightly wrapped rubber band, our horse looked like he was going to explode today and trounce this unsuspecting field of patsies.

Well, the gate opened and I noticed that the rider put the horse in a hold that resembled a full nelson to control the speed. The horse wanted to run, but the hold was so intense he looked as if he wanted to dump this rider and take off! Well, we did a good job I guess in taking him back as he spotted the field some 20 lengths or so. They turned for home, and the

florine.keus@content.nl

Marjolein Verkerk
Senior Consulent

marjolein.verkerk@content.nl

070-310 2124

# CONTENT
www.contentexecutive.nl

Korte Poten 55
2511 EC Den Haag
Tel. 070-312 19 31
Fax 070-312 19 30
www.content.nl

member of **USG** people

**CONTENT** ALS JIJ HET BENT

rider stopped choking the life and sprit out of the horse and let him finally run. While we were passing all the tired horses and finished sixth or so, the consensus amongst the trainer's entourage was that the rider let him loose just a little too late. Well, these horses are fickle if anything. Better late than never, and better sixth than dead last!

# EXCUSE 26
## "RACE WAS TOO LONG"

Your trainer takes you to the next upcoming public sale with the intention to "take a look and see" at some of the horses that he has earmarked in the sales catalogue as possible candidates for your next purchase. You are told that you need to have a horse that will run early as a two-year-old, so common sense should govern that you are there to buy a sprinter so the trainer can get some early dividends. The "look and see" almost always turns into a "must buy," and you take home the bargain of a lifetime!

Well, all that training and conditioning spells out that the horse wants to go a distance of ground for his first race. In trainer speak, the translation is that the horse is slow! (Which is why you were able to purchase him at less than half the price of that auction's sales average.)

Well, you wouldn't think that the horse was too slow, as on this day the horse found himself all alone on the lead. Never even considering the slow as molasses fractions the horses were running, you as the owner are thinking that your horse is blazing a trail on his way to a gate to wire victory.

Well, Mother Nature and genealogy quickly take over as the horse just can't run as far as the race was written.

Your horse finishes up the track. You are not terribly disappointed or surprised when the trainer acknowledges that the race was too long for this guy who was bred to be a sprinter. After all, he was still on the lead after six furlongs, and that's what he will have to run next time, right? Wrong!!! See excuse 27!

# EXCUSE 27
## "RACE WAS TOO SHORT"

Standing in the saddling area, watching your horse being displayed is quite a feeling. Everyone there thinks that their young horse is not only the best-looking horse in the race, but they all have that feeling that this is their day. Usually the trainer has all the logical reasons why you have a shot to win the race. The betting public, however, is not as gullible. With racing forms in hand they know what you should have known long before the race. You are way over your head! The racing secretary was generously kind while setting your odds at 12-1. I guess he also thinks giving owners some false expectations is good for the game. I mean, 12-1 means we have a good chance to win. At least that's what you think.

Well, the rider gets a leg up on your horse, and the instruction from the trainer is a simple "go to the front and improve your position." Sounded fairly logical to me. We did in fact go to the lead in the last Maiden Special Weight race and just couldn't hold on during the last quarter mile or so as "that race was too long."

Walking up to the betting window while your horse is in the post parade, you are as proud as you are excited. Never mind the horse is now 58 to 1 on the tote board. It's just more money for you when you go to collect on your winning ticket!

Well, as the handicappers expected, the fractions in this sprint were much faster than the horse was capable of running. We broke dead last and finished dead last, as all of the other horses got out in front of him and improved their positions away from him! The rider came off him saying that he had a nice stride, and the race was just too short!

Well, after feeling like the proverbial "cat who ate the canary" when placing my bet on this horse that was 58-1 because I thought no-one else was aware that the last time he ran he was on the lead after six furlongs, I suddenly get a case of dry mouth as I rip up the tickets and realize that this one is doomed for bottom level Maiden Claimers. Maybe it was the feathers of that canary that were hard to swallow and not the reality that this great bargain of a purchase is just a slow horse!

# EXCUSE 28
## "HATED THE INSIDE POST"

As a general rule, most young horses are not particularly fond of the inside post position. In one-turn races, the inside post is an obstacle and not an advantage despite what they taught you in physics class.

So you draw the inside post, and no one really tells you about the disadvantages and possible peril that Post Position 1 can bring when you are new and still naïve to racing horses. Most find out after the years of track tuition is paid that you would be better off scratching from any one-turn race when you draw the inside post position. Better to scratch and race another day than to become another statistic the handicappers use in their equations and evaluations of a race. So after the rider comes back from the race with the "nice horse, hated the post" routine, we should all know that this is not a creative excuse that needed to be dreamt up or stated ad hoc. He knew the second they left the gate and the horse saw the rail out of his left eye for as far as he could see and was tentative until whipped and scrubbed to run faster that when he returned this dead piece back to the trainer, the inside post excuse was going to be administered today!

# EXCUSE 29
## "HATED THE OUTSIDE POST"

    Running a longer race than all of his foes is not what a horse wants to do. Hence I am standing in the saddling area, making small talk with the rider (pardon the pun) and trainer when the rider starts talking strategy of how we can win the race from all the way out there! In some fantasy type scenario, the trainer tells him that there is plenty of speed to his inside, so "let's take back and make one run off the top of the stretch," stating the speed horses will tire as we are circling them off the turn. Sounds like a plan until the gate opens up and the horse bolts to the outside, looking for the gap in the fence and probably looking to get back to the barn and find his feed tub. Well, the rider does a magnificent job of getting him back to the racing part of the track and even passes a few tired horses by the time they hit the wire. Coming off the horse, we were given the words of encouragement of how much ground he covered once back on to the racing part of the track. If only we didn't have such a bad post position, as we are told he "hated the outside post."
    Between you and me, it was simply a case of the horse having more sense than all of us who fell asleep in this part of physics class in high school. Horses, albeit terribly nearsighted, have terrific peripheral vision. This horse must have seen the

finish line out of one eye and his barn out of the other and quickly surmised that it would be quicker to get to the barn than to the wire!! After all, the food is in the barn. Maybe they should put a feed tub in the winners circle for this guy next time he draws the outside post position!

# EXCUSE 30
## "HATED HORSES ON BOTH SIDES"

When a horse shies away from the rail or bolts to the outside fence, conventional wisdom tells you that a middle post would be the great equalizer, and your horse will display all of his honed skills and natural talents when the post position gods shine some light on you at the next draw, and assign you a post that would allow your horse to come out of the gate with a horse on each side of him. Trainers call this "covering up," as the horse is covered on both sides with no place to lug in or bolt out.

Well, as great as this sounds, some horses just don't care to have 1200 pounds of horseflesh leaning on them from both sides. Being naturally bred to run away from what they fear, "the cover up" didn't work out too well today. It actually backfired, as the horse just stopped and let the "leaners" run unmolested while falling into the back of the pack with nowhere to go. I mean, you can't take him outside as he will bolt. The opening on the rail is not an option as he hates that, too! Now what?

Well, the only "covering up" done today was when the rider covered up the fact that my horse was just not aggressive enough to be a competitive racehorse by proclaiming that he just "didn't like having horses on both sides!"

# EXCUSE 31
## "HORSE NEEDS GRASS"

No, not to eat, but to run on, as this horse wasn't made for the dirt surface, so I am now told. Usually you don't get this wonderful advice until after half a dozen or so attempts on the dirt. You know, a couple of tries without the blinkers, then the blinkers on, tongue tie, Lasix, and the bad luck excuses come first. After all other previous excuses are exhausted and the bills for this horse are finally choking the fun out of this game, you learn about something called "turf action." The rider usually gives the turf action prognosis to the trainer, and the trainer passes it along with the turf pedigree lesson in an envelope with the training bill. The turf action idea seems logical enough; you gladly pay the bill and tell yourself that the horse has good turf pedigree and turf action. You convince yourself that this venture is still not a totally wasted effort. Too bad it's November in New York or you wouldn't have to wait five months before seeing this plan result into a win photo and a little relief for the pocketbook!

# EXCUSE 32
## "TRACK WAS CUPPY"

The definition of a cuppy racing surface is basically a dry racetrack that is so arid that the sand caves in and falls in around a horse's footprint. This results in a cuppy craterlike hole rather than a hoof print. I think all horses dislike such a surface, but I must have had the ones that really hated such a race surface. I heard this excuse many times. I did know that there were horses bred for the grass, the mud, mile races, sprint races, routes, and everything in between. Now if someone would just figure out how to breed a "cupper," I would be the first buyer of such a breed!

# EXCUSE 33
## "TRACK WAS TOO HARD"

When you are standing on the rail and hear the thundering hooves, you really do think that this is all part of the excitement of thoroughbred horse racing. Never would you imagine that one day you may own a horse, and a rider will dismount in total disgust saying that his horse lost the race because the track was too hard. Hard racetracks usually result in faster running times. After all, a track that can double as a tarmac will really help shatter old racing records, and that's good for the sport. Sort of like juicing the baseball and moving in the fences to give baseball fans the excitement of seeing multiple home runs in a game.

Well, not all horses like this zip strip of a racetrack. As a matter of fact, my horses at times actually ran slower on this surface. They failed to tell me that the chips in the knees and ankles, which I still didn't know about, were banging around like a pinball against a cushion, causing the horse severe pain. The horse really didn't stop and shut down because the track was too hard! He just couldn't deal with the vibration of loose bones clanging around in those joint ligaments!

# EXCUSE 34
## "LIKES THE MUD"

A "mudder" is a horse that presumably likes the mud, as the past performance would show that this guy races better on a muddy or sloppy track surface. There are all types of handicapping methods that go into this thought process, even before the horse ever takes his first step on this type of surface. From genetic history to the size of the foot, a horse will be declared a possible "mudder" usually after failing on a regular or "fast" track. Lots of horses scratch out of races when the track comes up too wet. Not usually because these trainers fear the "mudder," but usually because their horses either hate the mud or are just too valuable to run on what is in reality a perilous surface. This all got me wondering. Is a mudder a horse that enjoys the hard concussion of a sloppy track, or perhaps they just love getting pelted with mud clumps in the face while in full stride? My guess is that they like the softer competition along with the normally smaller field. Or perhaps they aren't "mudders" at all. Maybe they are just not mud haters!

Horses may win on the mud despite the havoc that the mud shoes or caulks play on their joints. Ahh, maybe that's why those very expensive, well-bred horses scratched out of the race. They must be planning to race more than just once this year. Funny how that thought sets in only after you win the pot and realize three days later that it's only a loan. You see, after the trainer calls you to inform you that the horse came out of the race lame, and he needs some surgery along with some time off, the day of victory was really just a moral one. The financial stipend that just cleared in your account for the win will now be needed to take care of this horse for the next nine months! I guess it's like a loan! I think I should have named this one "Loan Me The Money"

# EXCUSE 35
## "HATED THE MUD"

See excuse # 34, but take the financial stipend out of the equation. This miscalculation results in the same outcome without the win purse money or picture!

The trainer and the betting public really liked his mud numbers, but this horse hated the jarring sensation in his knees and ankles and just stopped running in time to get hit in the eye with a clump of mud and a small stone. Now, not only do we have to fix the knees, but we also need to pay for the expensive medications and treatments in order to prevent us from having to remove the horse's eye. Not a good day!

# EXCUSE 36
## "HORSE GOT OUT"

During the race when a horse bears out while in stride, the rider or trainer will typically arrive at the conclusion, solely for the owner's ego, that the horse would have won the race except he "got out." This bit of news is meant to lead the owner to believe that the horse ran more ground than the others and maybe had an obstacle on the racecourse. Truth be known, horses usually bear out because they are running away from a sore leg. Bearing out is a horse's way of pulling away from the pain. Horses bear outward or inward, usually when they are so tired they just can not move forward in a straight line anymore. So the next time you lose a race due to your horse bearing out, beware. You should not expect to see the horse perform at this level for several months. Whether it be from poor conditioning or a leg injury, only lots of time and a healthy drop in competition will cure what ails him. The problem will not be remedied next week when the racing office calls looking for your horse to race, regardless of what your trainer tells you!

# EXCUSE 37
## "HORSE LUGGED IN"

See excuse # 36. Same problem. Different leg! "Lugging in" is just trainer speak for bearing inward because he only has three sound legs. Beware!

# EXCUSE 38
## "BAD KARMA IN THE BARN"

Before you laugh, please consider that trainers and backstretch employees are the most superstitious people you will ever meet. Being part of a culture that really doesn't know why horses win and don't win, they assume that everything comes down to luck and fate. This is how they justify long shots winning and favorites losing. Many of these people are constantly betting on losing horses but think of themselves as the great forecasters of the racing world as they rip up their losing tickets!

I once got yelled at by a legendary trainer for telling the jockey that I would see him in the winner's circle! Can you imagine the nerve of me making such a bold statement?

Well, this excuse, which we have numbered excuse #38, actually happened to me once in a stake race. We traveled to race out of state and out of our element. We flew down to Florida to run in a $100,000 ungraded stake contest and shipped the horse a week before the race. We flew our own jockey down to ride this horse, as the jockey had been on this horse in his last three starts and won with him twice. Everything was fine, and we were the overwhelming favorite. I guess flying down our own rider told everyone now we meant business. Well, when the gate opened up, the horse broke real slow and spotted the field a bunch of lengths. The field was big and the ground to be made up was not as big an obstacle as the wall of horses in front of us. Our horse, who was clearly the best, was weaving in and out of the wall of horses trying his best to get to the front. Well, the wire came up quicker than we could get to the front, and admirably, our horse ran second, which was no small feat as he ran an eighth mile farther than the rest of the field. Well, the rider came off stating the obvious, that we had the best horse in the race. So I said, tongue in cheek, that someone needs to tell that to the Horsemen's Bookkeeper because she is about to put the win money in the other owner's account. That's when I was told that we had bad racing luck, and it all started that morning when he noticed that people weren't getting along with each other in the barn! Bad karma, he called it! I kid you not.

# EXCUSE 39
## "RIDER LOST THE WHIP"

Yes, I know that stuff happens in the heat of the battle. Batters can lose the grip on a baseball bat, flinging it into a crowd. A running back can fumble away the football on the way to the goal line, and on and on.

But why does the rider only lose the whip in races that we would have won if he held on to it? We have been in plenty of races when we were never a threat. He always seemed to come back with the stick in hand on those days. So why did he have to be old butterfingers today when we had a shot?

I am really not sure if the whip is effective or not for all horses. This is and has always been a controversial issue. However, if the excuse is true to form and the rider losing the whip cost us the race as I was told, then shouldn't they be fined for losing the race due to losing the whip?

Where do you draw the line on intentional and unintentional fouls? Do you really think I feel better about this loss now that I know that the rider lost the whip in the stretch as soon as we were going to pass that other horse? I really don't need to hear this as an excuse again. If he can't hold the whip, then let's buy him a can of pine tar before we give him a leg up next time.

# EXCUSE 40
## "LOST A SHOE"

Horses lose shoes in races more than most would expect. Owners know this, as only the owner would be told such an important fact as a "soother" after losing a race. Typically, owners race their horses with optimism. Why shouldn't they be optimistic? After all, the trainers, who are expert and professional in this business, enter their horses in races they think they can win. At least you would think so, as this is a purely logical approach. The fact is, at the odds of 35-1, nobody but the owner thinks the horse has a chance to win the race. So at the conclusion of the race, owners leave the track feeling a bit like a deflated balloon, and await the trainer's telephone call later that evening to learn how the horse came out of the race. Well, the "lost a shoe" excuse is used as a buffer. It's sort of like saying, I know we ran awful out there, but we really don't know what we have, as he lost a shoe somewhere in the race and that changed everything. Now I am pretty sure the betters that made this horse 35-1 couldn't have possibly known that the horse would lose a shoe during the race. So why was he 35-1? The trainer suggested glue-on shoes. They are expensive, but hey, we will try anything, I say.

In the end I must confess that I have heard this lost a shoe nonsense more times than I care to admit. I used to ask the trainer if we could give the blacksmith a few extra bucks so he could use better and longer nails!

Oh and by the way, I have been told that we lost a shoe in races that we won, which filled me with the thoughts of having the next Citation in my barn...I mean, if he could win with only three shoes.

# EXCUSE 41
## "RUN DOWN"

The definition of a run down bandage is basically a patch that is applied to the legs so that the fetlocks won't hit the ground and scrape and bruise while galloping.

Horses that run down without the run down bandages or patches will come back after the race and bleed all over the place, even on the trainer's shoes. The rundown excuse must be legitimate, as the sight of all that blood is enough to tell one that it must hurt!

# EXCUSE 42
## "GRABBED HIS QUARTER"

Another visually disturbing picture that includes horses bleeding all over the trainer's shoes! Horses sometimes leave the gate looking a little mangled and uncoordinated, causing one shoe to step on the other foot, or quarter as they are called, ripping a good piece of flesh and foot right off. This is another situation that seems innocent enough and certainly warrants an excuse for losing a race. The problem is that the unsuspecting owner doesn't realize that, in most cases, this can be prevented with proper shoeing and training from the starting gate. Once it happens, the injury is so painful and debilitating that the horse won't race without pain for several months.

# EXCUSE 43
## "HOT NAILED IN THE A.M."

As ridiculous as it may sound, horses will sometimes be shod in the morning of a race. If you were going out to dance, run in a marathon, or even play some basketball, would you wear new shoes to do so? Probably not.

Well, that good old farrier will from time to time "hot nail" a horse while shoeing them in the morning. Of course the horse is fine with the nail in the tender part of the foot, until he has to race on it, and the pain and infection set in. Like having a stone in your shoe, I suppose; you might be able to walk with it, but running is out of the realm of all possibilities. Has anyone ever considered that shoeing a horse the day of the race, after, in fact, the track vet inspects him for soundness, leaves too much room for shenanigans? Now I am not saying that farriers are not to be trusted. I am saying that when it comes to this high-stakes game, no one should be beyond suspicion!

In fact, I have not met a farrier I didn't like. However, knowing that accidents can sometimes be premeditated when money and gambling are involved, I would think it best to eliminate all doubt by banning such maintenance on race day.

# EXCUSE 44
## "NEEDS CAULKS"

A mud caulk is a type of shoe that a horse can wear on his feet. Mud caulks have stickers or points on the shoes that give the horse better traction, regardless of the plethora of injuries they can cause on knees and hocks. There are some tracks that legend says you can't win on unless you wear the mud caulks or stickers. Frankly, it's because of the legend that all the competition is wearing them and the "when in Rome" philosophies take over, and caution is thrown to the wind.

I learned early on that in most cases mud caulks will let you win the battle but lose the war. What good is winning a race if the purse pot will not be large enough to carry the horse for the lay-up time involved after sustaining the injuries he will suffer due to the caulks? Trainers, of course, do not give you back their winning percentage proceeds. So don't expect help when you need more money to cover the horse's lay-up time. You are on your own to pay the piper. Your horse will run noticeably better the first time he runs with caulks, so be prepared to hear the I told you so's!

# EXCUSE 45
## "DIDN'T LIKE THE CAULKS"

    Well, after you heed your trainer's advice and put the caulks on your horse, your horse, as I stated in excuse # 44, will undoubtedly run better than he did last time. Good enough to run second or third in some cases.

    Now you're moving up the ladder, so to speak, as the caulks on in the last race made your ninth place finish two races back a distant memory. Based on the fact that you ran third last time out with the caulks on, you find yourself as the owner of the favorite this time out. You feel ever so confident that the betting public is right this time in making you the overwhelming favorite to win this contest.

    Your horse looks like a winner until he hits the turn, and all of a sudden his stride gets shorter and shorter as the other horses get farther and farther ahead of him. Jogging in a teacup is a much used expression that comes to mind. The beaten favorite, always subject to real disappointment and the occasional booing fan, makes you feel a little embarrassed. So what happened here today? The trainer is scratching his head as the rider hops off and tells the trainer that the horse should be checked, as he felt a "little short and choppy underneath." The vet takes a look and can't find anything (except an invoice for you); thus the trainer tells you that he might not have liked the caulks as much as he originally thought. Let's take them off next time, he proclaims. Translation: We can not find the chip yet that the caulks most probably created in his last race. So let's take the caulks off to prevent further damage. Maybe we can keep this guy in the barn until we find you a new one to take his stall! When in doubt of a trainer's commission, day money is the next best thing.

# EXCUSE 46
## "RIDER STOPPED WHIPPING"

Whipping a horse that is clearly tired and finished running is basically cruel and unusual punishment. So when your horse is backing up and the rider wraps up on him, presuming that the competition is over his head, this should be a good sign that the rider is doing the right thing. There is no sense in beating him senseless for fifth place money. You as an owner should be appreciative of the rider's humanitarian approach.

Until the trainer tells you that, now we really don't know how good or bad the horse is, as the rider wrapped up on him too early, and the 13 losing lengths is not an accurate gauge of whether the horse belongs in this company or not. The humanitarian effort has now become an excuse and fodder for some sort of conspiracy theory, and you as an unsuspecting owner actually start to believe it! Your mind starts to gather hope that you will win next time with a hungrier rider!

As if the horse and trainer had nothing to do with this abysmal effort.

# EXCUSE 47
## "HORSE HATED BEING HIT"

The mere inference that a horse likes being whipped is enough to make one's head spin. Hence the thought that your horse might lose a race if he does get the whip is something out of a P.T. Barnum anecdote.

I have been told that the horse was whipped too many times and resented the whip, which is why he just let the other horses pass him. Spiteful horse I have here, I thought. The joke must be on me then that the other horses in the race enjoyed being pummeled by leather and they couldn't wait to get to the wire first. Where in the breeding line do I find the stallion with masochist genes?

# EXCUSE 48
## "HORSE WAS SHORT"

    Everything is hunky dory as your horse is contesting the early pace for the lead, and it is looking like today's the day to finally take a win picture. All of a sudden the horse stops running, and you start hoping to finish second, third, hold on for fourth, get a little something for fifth, and in the blink of an eye you pass the finish line beating just one horse. To boot, that horse you passed had to be pulled up and now awaits the track ambulance to van him off the track. Rider comes off the horse and proclaims that the horse was just a little short today. The trainer agrees and shares with you the fact that the horse was short, hoping that you may not know that short means that the horse was insufficiently trained to run the distance he was entered to run at today.

    Maybe you should short the training bill when this excuse comes up. That'll at least let the trainer know that you have an idea what "short "actually means! And now, so does he.

# EXCUSE 49
## "LOST STIRRUP"

    Like excuse # 39, stuff happens. Lose a whip, a rider's foot falls out of a stirrup, it's an imperfect world! I am still not sure, though, that this means we would have won if we didn't fall out of the stirrup. What I do know is that there are no do-overs in this game. All of the money and time lost can not be replaced nor refunded. The rider gets paid no matter what! This is when you wonder why an owner who actually contributes his money and product to actually put on this fantastic and profitable show doesn't get paid to do so. Hmmm… Let's name one "Union Organizer."

# EXCUSE 50
## "BLED"

The obvious bleeder comes off the track with blood gushing out of his nostrils, sometimes caused by lung hemorrhaging. While this is a huge and frightening concern, it is usually not the time when you will hear this as an excuse. I mean, if the animal is spewing blood profusely, it's really more of a situation than an excuse.

This excuse is usually used a little more innocuously. Your horse loses a race and goes back to the barn and awaits the vet to stick a scope through his nostril. The iota or speck of blood found in the mucous membrane is what becomes excuse # 50. It is remedied by either Lasix for the first time or an increase in the dosage of Lasix if he is already on the stuff. Please refer to excuse # 12 and excuse # 13 to predict what will probably occur next

# EXCUSE 51
## "SADDLE WAS TOO LOOSE"

When the horse arrives in the saddling area, the horse and the trainer are met by a valet that delivers the saddle and assists the trainer in affixing the saddle and "tacking up" the horse. They normally pull the girth around the horse as if they were trying to put 1,200 pounds of horseflesh into a size 34 waist pair of blue jeans. This should be a fairly simple and foolproof procedure. Sort of like fastening the lug nuts on your car after having the tires changed. Routine should be the word of the day here. Well, not so fast! I have actually been told that the rider couldn't get into the horse on the turn as the saddle was improperly affixed and became loose and dangerous. Just another failed attempt to win this condition, probably because he has lost so much weight from being improperly nourished. Perhaps this regiment of racing every six days has taken a little bit of flesh off his bones. It's not like the horse wasn't fit enough, mind you. Maybe he was too fit and that's why the belt was loose! I will tell you that I now do check to make sure the garage properly fastened my lug nuts when I get my brakes or tires repaired. Hey, you never know!

# EXCUSE 52
## "SADDLE WAS TOO TIGHT"

See excuse # 51 and add a few pounds to the horse. Could you run with a belt that was too tight? Would you blame the belt or your newfound protruded waist?

Too loose, too tight...it's all the same if you ask me. The trainers I guess are subject to be stronger on some days than others while tightening the saddle and girth. Either way, this is a really lame excuse, but trust me, you will not only hear it someday, but you'll buy it hook, line, and sinker! After you buy the excuse, you will be buying the hot pepper spray the trainer needs to put on the bedding in the horse's stall. What did you think, that the hay belly is helping?

# EXCUSE 53
## "TEETH NEED TO BE DONE"

Actually, as crazy as it sounds the first time you hear this excuse, the more logical the reasoning gets as you learn more about this game. Who would think that the horse that just bolted to the outside fence or blew the turn did so because he needed some general dentistry? However, once you consider the importance of the horse's mouth relative to steering him, it becomes fairly evident that if the teeth are bugging him or are too sharp, needing some attention, it is possible that the blown turn was all in the mouth and not in the legs. Of course the compelling question has to be asked as to why hasn't anyone noticed this until race day! More compelling is the question of what horse the dentist actually did last week that you were billed for. I hope it wasn't cosmetic! At this rate he will not be smiling for a camera anytime too soon!

# EXCUSE 54
## "FEET NEED TO BE DONE"

In order for a horse to be capable of performing at his optimum, he will need his feet to be trimmed at the most suitable hoof angle for the individual's size and conformation. At least that's what most so-called, self-professed experts think. The problem is that most farriers like to trim and shoe without much thought of the individual horse. Kind of like a hitting instructor trying to teach every player how to hit a home run, regardless of the individual's size or strength. Like most athletes, horses need to be looked upon as individuals and treated as such. Improper angles either cut or left unattended lead to more serious injuries and ultimately breakdowns.

When you lose a race and no other problem can be identified, trainers often call in the cavalry to do a complete makeover on your animal. Feet being improperly trimmed is always a last resort excuse. One would be curious why it took until the injury or worse, the breakdown, to identify that the hoof angle was all wrong and a contributing factor to the losses. The blacksmith practically lives in the barn, so hasn't anyone told this guy the "ounce of prevention" line yet?

# EXCUSE 55
## "JUMPED A SHADOW"

A shadow roll is a fuzzy band that goes over a horse's nose and below his eyes, preventing the horse from actually seeing the ground beneath him. Horses will jump over their own shadows as well as shadows from the poles and rails of the racetrack itself. I have had several horses that all of a sudden changed their gait for no apparent reason during a particular time of the year. The trainers will ready themselves for the excuses based on the sun positioning and the creation of shadows during that particular time of the day. Shadow rolls are a good idea when the horse jumps a shadow. This is also a page out of the "ounce of prevention" book as horses that jump shadows can become downright dangerous to those around them.

# EXCUSE 56
## "DOESN'T LIKE THE HEAT"

    As logical as jumping shadows is a legitimate excuse for losing a race, it's as illogical that the horse you own only likes the cold weather and can't stand the heat. Oh, we've all heard this before about horses that we have that ran so well all year not doing well in the summertime. After a couple of years of taking my horses that competed all winter and spring from Aqueduct to Saratoga just to pay more money to be there and pretend to enjoy losing, I came to one irrefutable conclusion. It's not the heat but the competition that is beating my string of horses. Someone might want to tell the trainer who is trying to convince you that your horses like the cold weather and the weather will cool at the end of the meet. Remember, though, that your horses are his ticket to spend the month of August away from home at your expense. You, too, would come up with a good excuse in order to get an all-expense-paid trip to paradise and get to call it a business trip!

# EXCUSE 57
## "HATES THE COLD"

Well, most of us hate the cold weather. Here in New York, horse owners and trainers all hope for an early winter even though they really despise the cold weather. You see, it's not that we have horses that love the cold weather. It's just a lot easier to win here when all the good horses and high-profile trainers take off to sunny Florida for less purse money and higher expenses for their extraordinarily wealthy owners who do this for fun!

Well, here in the Northeast the winter brings a plethora of purses and slow horses, so we'd be crazy to not be beating the drums for an early winter. Especially after the drubbing we took in Saratoga this year! Well, that is all contingent on the fact that your horses are the types that don't hate the cold weather. Imagine after starting this horse as a two-year-old in early spring and racing him through the summer to get drubbed by the big boys, the November winds blow in at the same time as the big boys blow out of the state, chasing the sunshine, when you again finish up the track for the eighth time in the horse's young career. Well, you will be given one excuse after the other, just keeping you in the game long enough to get past the year when you will be told in early February that perhaps your horse just hates the cold weather. Well, the warmer weather is coming, and maybe you can squeak in a win before the Florida snowbirds get back!

# EXCUSE 58
## "DOESN'T LIKE RACING UNDER THE LIGHTS..."

    Night racing offers new opportunities as well as new problems, thus a whole new variety of excuses. From hearing about your horse's disdain for the lights, the moon, the cooling off of temperature, the dew on the grass etc., you will be faced with a new concept of why your horse lost the race tonight.

    One time in a nighttime stake race at The Meadowlands Racetrack, my horse ran a solid third to a very nice multiple stakes winner. After the race, my rider told me we would have beaten the winner if we had some night racing experience. I then asked the rider if the lights bothered the horse, and he told me that it was either the bright lights or the crescent moon that cost us the race. Now I can identify with the guy who coined the phrase about "winning once in a blue moon." His horse must not have liked crescent moons, either!

# EXCUSE 59
## "GOT SPOOKED BY THE CROWD"

    Horses are curious creatures with tremendous peripheral vision and remarkable hearing. So it should not be a shock for anyone to consider that a horse might get "spooked" by a large, noisy crowd. Whether it be in the post parade or when turning for home, the noise can and will spook a horse. I once had a horse that blew the turn heading for the stretch so bad that it looked as if he could have grabbed a hot dog and a soda from one of the railbirds rooting his horse home.
    Afterwards I was told that the horse probably blew the turn and headed for the crowd as the grandstand noise might have spooked him.
    Funny, I thought horses ran from their fears. Perhaps this guy was just a friendly kind of horse and wanted to grace his presence to the grandstand fans. Well, it turned out that the horse never raced again. No, it wasn't the stage fright that prevented the horse from running again. It was the slab fracture in his knee that finally stopped this horse from future competition. Wait...do you think that perhaps the fractured knee had anything to do with the horse wanting to grab a hot dog and soda on the way to the finish line in his last race? Kind of like an encore presentation. Let's name this one "Farewell, I'm Done."

# EXCUSE 60
## "NEEDS TO RELAX"

Funny thing this horse racing business is at times. A horse is raised on a high-octane diet, with more performance-enhancing drugs than even the baseball players are reportedly using nowadays, taught to be aggressive when busting out of the gate and running pedal to the metal when seeing the whip. Only to now be a victim of losing the race because he wasn't relaxed enough to win a race. Your bills will be dominated with all of these rocket fuel supplements, muscle and body builders, corn oils, etc. So relaxation is really not part of the diet!

# EXCUSE 61
## "ANKLES ARE BUGGING HIM"

The toe grabs, the mud caulks, and all the other shoeing that creates a jarring effect will sooner or later lead to some sort of debilitating injury. Ankles bugging your horse is a cry for help and a reason, more than it is an excuse for his poor performance. This excuse will ultimately lead to countless x-rays, obscene vet bills, and suggestions for some voodoo-like cures.

Fact is that whether you use any of the voodoo-like cures or the typical useless cures of blistering or firing, the only thing that will heal your horse is time. Lots of time! All the prescribed cures that are intended to keep your horse in the trainer's stall, with the hopes of not missing more than a race or two, is nothing more than wishful thinking!

# EXCUSE 62
## "KNEES ARE BUGGING HIM"

See excuse # 61 and add to the voodoo and mythical cures the injections of steroids and corticosteroids into the fray. All suggestions of quick fixes should be taken with a grain of salt. In fact, steroid injections in the knee will not only create more damage, but will actually inhibit the healing process. The tap, inject, and drop the horse in company approach will not make him a better horse. It all comes along with all types of possible horrific consequences that can result in death to not only your horse, but the riders in the race. Proceed with caution when you hear this excuse and the plan to fix it.

# EXCUSE 63
## "SHINS ARE BUGGING HIM"

Sore and buck shins are a common excuse used by trainers particularly in younger horses. Trainers use this excuse as if an owner should expect all young horses to ultimately have this problem.

Once we had a horse that was developing into a fine athlete and potential money-maker. The barn was so excited about this guy that we were getting Derby fever before he even had his first race. So with all of the common sense of a houseplant, we rushed this horse to the races early in his two-year-old career. After all, conventional wisdom tells us that Derby hopefuls need to be well seasoned before they reach their three-year-old careers. As an owner, it is difficult to not get caught up in the rush to get the horse to the races as soon as possible.

Well, we ran a very good second in our first start in a competitive field at Belmont Park. We couldn't wait to race him at Saratoga Racetrack on opening weekend. It didn't seem to matter that the horse would have to race on inadequate rest. We were going to show the upper echelon of the racing world what we had in our barn. Guess what? We won! Oh what a feeling. The trainer was I-told-you-so-ing everyone at the track that day and night. What was the difference, I ignorantly asked. Well, it turns out that we used a shoe in the race called a "toe grab." Sounds innocent enough; besides, we won, so that was the point! Unfortunately in the next race the horse ran a half of a mile in a mile race and just stopped like he was hog-tied.

The next morning in a very matter of fact way, the trainer told me that the horse's shins were bugging him, and he thought we may have a case of bucked shins. The cure I am told is some type of topical concoction that will bring the buck, or swelling, down in no time. Sounds to me like this is a small problem, especially when the vet tells me it is a very common ailment amongst young horses. Well, two weeks off became three months, and I couldn't help but to further investigate the matter.

Well, it turns out that a bucked shin is trainer speak for a fractured shin. The cause has more to do with negligent training than Mother Nature. The toe grabs contributed to the high level of concussion that created the remodeling and subsequent fracture of the bone.

Well, we never did get to the Derby. I guess one could argue that we just didn't have a Derby caliber horse. I guess we will never really know! I wonder how many other horses are out there that we will never know about!

# EXCUSE 64
## "FEET ARE BUGGING HIM"

Quarter cracks, hot nails, abscesses, bad trimming, navicular diseases, etc. Stuff happens and you better get used to it! Foot problems bring on some of the wildest cures and suggested remedies that you will ever hear. So there is some comic relief, I guess. I once had a trainer tell me that we needed to pack the foot in a Brillo-like compound for 48 hours. However, that didn't come close to the trainer who wanted to inject the horse's foot nerve with snake oil to kill the nerve and deaden the pain. Ever really think that there is really such thing as a snake oil salesman? Well, in this business there are more than a few.

I do wonder sometimes, though, if you were to take eight horses with bad feet and chronic foot problems and put them all in the same race, would the winning trainer still think that the horse's feet are still bugging him?

# EXCUSE 65
## "JUST NOT RIGHT TODAY"

    This is trainer speak for "Houston, we have a problem," but they just haven't identified it yet. Don't worry, though, because after the blood tests, scoping, x-rays, chiropractic advice, and a whole myriad of tonics and potions, you will sooner or later find out why the horse was just not right today!

# EXCUSE 66
## "WASHED OUT IN THE GATE"

Usually the profuse sweating starts in the paddock and saddling area. While you and your trainer might be oblivious to this clearly visible and obvious dilemma, the betting public will not overlook the problem. Your horse will go from the odds of 5-2 up to 10-1 in a New York minute. You see, the bettors are more aware of the obvious as they have no emotional or financial attachments to your horse. The fact is that a horse that is shivering and sweating bullets because of nerves will most likely not perform well. When you hear this excuse immediately after a race, the only thought that should come to your mind is "Why is my horse so scared?" If in fact he is sound and has been properly trained, he should be ready and enthusiastic about running around that oval today. Perhaps he has had some less than kind experiences with the gate crew. Or, worse, if this horse is a seasoned pro and all of a sudden shows signs of being worried, perhaps he just doesn't want to break down or feel the pain of the injury he has and you don't know about. Back to the drawing board! At your expense, of course. The chalk is expensive in this business!

# EXCUSE 67
## "DIDN'T SWEAT AT ALL"

Sometimes horses are referred to as non-sweaters. Most of the time it has something to do with the climate change and the balance of hydration and the electrolytes in his system. This is why athletes drink sport drinks and take IVs to alleviate cramping.

While this problem is certainly a reason to lose a race on a given day, it will not prevent your horse from competing next time if the proper diet and electrolyte balance are maintained.

One time I had a horse go off as the even money favorite in Florida. The horse spent his career racing in New York, and it was not working out well here, so we decided to send him to easier races and lesser competition. Well, the horse lost the race, and the trainer in Florida called me to blame me for not telling him the horse was a so-called "non-sweater." Imagine blaming the owner for his blunder. Sort of like getting yelled at by the chef at a restaurant when you tell the waiter that you weren't happy with your meal. The irony here was that the Florida trainer actually broke and trained the horse as a yearling and as a two-year-old. He should have known the horse and how he would handle the heat better than anyone else. I suspect, though, that this was a case of one making their offense their best defense.

Oh, and by the way, the horse referred to here, never raced again. She was a filly that we decided to send to the breeding shed after the non-sweat race. No, not because the horse was a so-called non-sweater, but because of the big chip in her ankle that we found out about shortly after the race! You haven't lived until you have heard trainers blaming other trainers for sending them bad horses. This must be how the great "Buckpasser" got his name!

# EXCUSE 68
## "NEEDS WRAPS"

Wraps, or bandages as they are called, are used on a horse's legs to prevent injury. However, most of the time they are there to prevent another trainer from seeing if there is a problem with the horses or not. At least a problem that can be visually noticed in the saddling area if not for the wraps. In claiming races, it's best to keep them guessing. It also prevents the track vet from seeing some obvious injury like a blown or thick suspensory ligament. If such an injury is seen by the track vet, they will scratch the horse at the gate. Better to risk life and limb and race this horse than to leave him in the barn collecting dust, and expenses. Hey, you never know; he may get claimed. One man's garbage is truly another man's gold. At least that's what he thinks right now!

So when your trainer tells you the horse needs wraps, beware. They will have nothing to do with the horse's overall racing performance, other than the fact that he will get by the track vet. If we knew this was going to happen, we would have named him "Blind Man's Bluff"!

# EXCUSE 69
## "DIDN'T LIKE THE WRAPS"

Horses typically don't like anything wrapped on their legs and will try their best to get the bandages off. I have watched horses eat the wraps off, even with Tabasco sauce painted on the bandage as a deterrent.

Again, while the excuse has been used countless times, the wraps whether on or off will make no difference in the outcome of the race. But if taking them off gives you hope, then I guess at least someone will feel better about the drubbing your horse just took in the race. Too bad you actually thought they would help today or else the horse may have been somewhere else where he may belong. You would have saved yourself a few bucks.

# EXCUSE 70
## "HATED THE COLOR OF THE WRAPS"

Front wraps or bandages come in all colors. I heard this excuse once when the rider proclaimed that the horse was looking down at his legs, and when the sun glared off the wraps the horse held his breath and lost a step.

I kid you not, the rider actually told us to use different colors next time. And we listened! Stupid is what stupid does comes to mind now. Now there is a new name for a racehorse that is as fitting as I have ever heard.

# EXCUSE 71
## "RAN INTO A BRICK WALL"

Well, we didn't really run into a brick wall! However, after running out of the myriad of excuses for this horse that always just stopped running during his races, it was refreshing to hear something original. Remember that the comedic value is worth the training expense to the eternal optimists. After all else fails—blinkers, Lasix, tongue ties, and all the various excuses and subsequent remedies—this excuse is at least the most telling. Stop wasting your money and get a new horse!

# EXCUSE 72
## "CAN'T HANDLE THE MENTAL PRESSURE OF BEING A RACEHORSE"

You think I am kidding, right? I had to have made this up! Wrong...This was told to me and most likely countless other disappointed owners when a horse is just making the trainer look bad.

Imagine that. While all of these horses are bred to race, I had to pick the one that wasn't mentally prepared to be the best that he can be. What bad luck, I thought to myself when I was told this about a horse that I thought looked the part of a winner. Funny how it took two years of training this guy, not to mention the tens of thousands of dollars spent, only to find this out now. Perhaps I should bring a horse psychologist along with the vet squad next time we are planning to buy a horse.

# EXCUSE 73
## "TOO INTELLIGENT"

The first time I heard this as an excuse (and I have heard it more than once), I was as confused as I was excited. You must understand that it takes a new owner several years and lots of lost races, along with three-quarters of a million dollars in tuition, before we learn anything.

So your horse runs fairly evenly the whole race, never really losing ground but never really trying to win the race, either. After the race is over and you finish a very dull fourth or fifth out of a field of ten, the rider hops off and says the horse never really tried out there today as he is pretty intelligent and spent the whole race running cautiously and protecting himself.

Well, all kinds of proud papa feelings come over you. Since you don't know any better, you think that your horse was just complimented on his intelligence. Like telling people about your youngster's report card. It's a proud moment when you tell your cronies that the rider said your horse had brains, as they are ripping up their win tickets.

It doesn't really dawn on you until much later on in your horse owner education process that the horse wasn't as intelligent as he was opposed to pain. You see, something told that horse on that day that the tear in his suspensory or chip in his ankle, which no one saw until after two months of training bills and two more dull races, might break him down for real if he tried any harder!

# EXCUSE 74
## "TOO LOOPY"

Not, I suppose, a term of endearment, but better than saying that the horse is just flat out crazy and is going to kill someone. Again, I have heard this one countless times—just don't know why no one noticed until after the race! The 20 months of training expenses that we have into her thus far would make you think that this shouldn't have been such a huge surprise.

# EXCUSE 75
## "CAN'T RUN WITH THESE"

Ah, finally an excuse that makes sense! Not all horses are created equally, and certainly this game would be no fun if they were. All of the formulas and opinions in picking out a horse on pedigree, conformation, size, and all of the nouveau nicking schemes still guarantee nothing when it comes to racing. That's the only reason why anyone would get involved.

When I hear this as an excuse, I sigh a breath of relief. No more excuses! A real reason why we lost!

Now if we would have just realized this in the beginning, we may have at least had the good sense to cut bait, drop the horse into a cheap claimer, and move into a better investment that might have given us more than the 13 excuses and 20 races we have into her. (Not to once again mention the thousands of dollars spent.) But I am still learning!

# EXCUSE 76
## "SPEED WAS HOLDING"

Well, we all have heard the saying that "pace makes the race." This is fodder for some brain-crushing to be done by the handicappers to try to figure out the outcome of a race. We have seen horses steal races at all levels by getting loose on the lead on a track where speed was holding, as they say. Problem is that sometimes your horse, which has proven to be a dead closer, may end up in a race on a track that is holding for speed. As your luck will have it, there will be only one horse in the race that has front end speed. Invariably this horse will get loose on the lead, and your even money closer will make his big move, only to pass all of the other's, but not quite catch the speed horse. Even though the past performances of this horse show that this horse should have folded like a cheap suit at the eighth pole, the rider always comes off the second place finisher in a race like this begging to ride the horse back next time. While this is a legitimate reason or excuse to lose a race, it does not mean you are a lock next time. See excuse # 77!

# EXCUSE 77
## "SPEED WASN'T HOLDING"

So here you are back to the races with your horse who was the second place finisher in his last start. Everyone is just gushing with confidence because that elusive trip to the winner's circle is now only a few minutes away. The rider is talking about the horse as if it has been all he has thought about in the last two weeks. The trainer gives him the pre-race instructions, and with complete and utter confidence and disregard he says to the rider, "This time break sharp, go to the lead, and just keep improving your position." Sounds like a plan. Too bad he is the odds on favorite, or it would be a real party after the race!

Well, the horse breaks sharp and finds himself in on the lead. Victory should surely be ours on this glorious day! Problem is that there is another speed horse in the race, and he is the 1a part of the entry, the rabbit. He is now making your horse work real hard on the front end, and by the time you come off the turn to enter the stretch you realize that for you to win, you will be setting the track record as the fractions so far have been sizzling. Well, the eighth pole comes up at about the same time your horse is laboring on his "hands and knees" just to finish the race. Your horse and the "rabbit" finish in last and next to last. Now it comes to you that pace makes the race, and you were just outpaced, out-raced, and out-thought by a very crafty trainer.

# EXCUSE 78
## "HATES TO BE RUSHED"

Some horses just like to leave the gate at their leisure and hate to be asked to run too hard too soon. I suppose they want to run when they feel like running. Well, these types of horses very rarely make a rider look smart. When the rider tries to make up the seven lengths that he and the horse spotted the field because of the slow break, he best not try to get it all back in the first quarter mile of the race. More often than not, the rider will try to get it all back, and you will hear excuse # 78!

Someone once said that most horses only have one run in them. I have concluded that rushing the horse up after a slow start is not exactly the one run you need to win the race!

# EXCUSE 79
## "HATES TO BE RESTRAINED"

Grabbing a hard hold of a horse and wrestling him into submission isn't the answer here, either. Sometimes a horse uses twice as much energy trying to run out of that full nelson than if he would have just been let loose and settled down evenly. Now I am not saying that letting him run full-bore from the gate is desirable. What I am saying is that it doesn't seem logical to take the horse out of the race so soon. Asking him to expend that much energy fighting with his rider just to stay well behind the pack is not the recipe for a good performance. A rider needs to be like a baseball or football player and employ the "soft hands" technique. When you get to hear this excuse for the first time, you will have already been thinking it. It's that obvious.

# EXCUSE 80
"HATES TO PASS HORSES"

This is a serious problem! The charts usually read "hung" on a horse like this {see excuse #5} but this is actually much more disheartening.

I once had a horse finish a race dead last. Well, actually I have had lots of horses finish dead last! The rider came off telling us that he had "a lot of horse" underneath him, but he just didn't want to catch up to anything. Now, I hate to sound like an alarmist, but this doesn't sound like a money-maker to me. Well, after he ran up the track so many times that the racing office threatened to ban him from the track, we moved him to a cheaper track. No, not because we thought that he could win there. After all, our advisers told us he doesn't like to pass other horses, so we moved him there because the training bills were cheaper! Truth be told, we needed some financial relief! Well, as it turns out, he competed a little better up there. Never did win a race, but did run a couple of thirds and fourths in fields bigger than three and four horses. I suspect it wasn't that he didn't like to pass horses after all. My guess is that he just couldn't pass the other horses, and they spared me the news.

# EXCUSE 81
## "HATES THE NEW BIT"

    Trainers are always looking for new equipment and such that will turn your bad investment to a winner. The eternal optimism in the trainers can be contagious. You as an owner will buy the new equipment excuse hook, line, and sinker. You will also end up buying the new equipment, too. No, you don't get it back when you leave. All new equipment becomes the property of the barn immediately after it's deemed ineffective.
    One time we had a horse blow the turn so bad that we thought she couldn't make left turns. Turns out that we just needed a new bit. Well, very predictably she lost again, and this time the reason was that she was paying too much attention to the new bit, which she apparently just didn't like.
    Yes, you guessed it. It was the big ol' chip in her knee and not the new bit that made it difficult to make sharp and crisp left turns! The trainer, bless his heart, did get another couple starts out of me or should I say the horse.

# EXCUSE 82
## "RAN OUT OF ROOM"

With racecourses being as long and wide as they are, you would never think that you could run out of room. Running out of room is more of a phenomenon than an excuse—like the traffic jam for no reason on the highway when you're in a "rush" to get to visit your in-laws.

It was a beautiful spring afternoon at beautiful Belmont Park. Wide and lush sweeping turns on the outside grass course makes it appear to be fit for a 28-horse field. Well, they don't run 28-horse fields here, ever. This was a field of eight first-level allowance horses. Room shouldn't be an issue, you would think.

Well after being blocked, bumped, and checked, we finally found some room on the inside rail turning for home. The leader was just three in front, and you know how grass horses usually close. Well, someone should have told our rider that the horse to beat was never going to let him get inside. There we go, gobbling up ground like Ms. Pacman, just to have to check the horse and try to swing outside, where there was some oncoming traffic. As I said, you know how these grass races finish.

We ran a very respectable third and actually could have won the race, I thought. Fully expecting the rider to come off the horse and say that he made a tactical error, or at least say that the horse wouldn't go through the hole on the inside, I was floored by what is now excuse # 82. He said he ran out of room!

Saying that he ran out of room is like someone saying that it wasn't their fault that their car struck a tree because they honked the horn but the tree never moved!

# EXCUSE 83
## "RAN OUT OF RACETRACK"

Have you ever heard the track announcer say "saved by the wire" in a close race when the horse on the lead is just holding on by a thread as the closer is coming?

Well, for every time you have heard "saved by the wire," there is a second place finisher being told that the horse just "ran out of racetrack."

# EXCUSE 84
## "RAN OUT OF TRAINER AT THE 16TH POLE"

Blessed is the trainer who admits he trained a short horse! It was just refreshing to hear a trainer actually blame his training techniques for the reason you got beat today by running just three-quarters of a mile in a six-and-a-half-furlong race.

I was all prepared to go take a picture. I was wet as I slid down the wet pavement, rooting my horse to the wire on a rainy day. As they passed me at the 16th pole, I noticed that our lead was dwindling and so was the horse's stride. It was like he was taking baby steps. I am sure I outran him to the line. So wet and bruised, I gathered myself together and went to see that we finished third. That would be good except that we had a six-length lead at the eighth pole. Well, the trainer either took pity on me and hung the blame on his training, or maybe he just kept me in the game for at least another race. The cynic in me says it's the latter that induced him into taking the blame.

# EXCUSE 85
## "NEEDS WIDER TURNS"

There are a lot of racetracks that are referred to as "bull rings" and "paper clip" tracks. Both with hairpin turns so sharp that only riders with in-depth experience of that particular track know how to win and stay safe at the same time. It's always tempting to bring your rider to these types of tracks, but the house riders usually excel at these ovals. Riders come back from these races thoroughly convinced that the hairpin turns were the reason the horse just lost. I am not so sure in these cases whether it's the plane or the pilot, but either way it'll always be the track's fault. Blaming the trainer, rider, or horse can result in disheartened, nonpaying owners. So it must be the track!

# EXCUSE 86
## "HE RAN AS FAR AS HE COULD"

Really? I have heard this, and I am still speechless…

# EXCUSE 87
### "HE RAN AS FAST AS HE COULD"

Still speechless. When I heard excuses 86 and 87 together, I almost wet myself. I have actually heard them together. What brilliance! What a great observation! What is everyone talking about when they say this is a tough business? My trainer has got it all down to a science... My horse just lost, but he ran as far as he could and as fast as he could.

# EXCUSE 88
## "NEEDS SOME TIME OFF"

No, not on a farm unless you have another horse to take the stall space. No, now you will pay the training bills but have no chance to even sniff a purse for awhile as your horse gets his rest and relaxation at the beautiful racetrack.

The horse only had 17 starts this year, and his form is deteriorating, so it must be time to regroup and take some time off. Another obvious reason and not an excuse. Oh, have no fear, you will hear this one several times a year. Better to pay and not lose I think may be the philosophy here.

# EXCUSE 89
## "NEEDS TO BE RUN RIGHT BACK"

Your horse just lost for the third time in 11 days. But he is getting closer to the winning horse. A fifth place finish, a fourth, and a third place finish. It would almost appear that the more the horse races, the better he is getting. Heaven forbid it would have something to do with breaking your horse's maiden by attrition theory that I shared in a previous excuse. It must be all the action he is seeing under the tutelage of your trainer.

Now you have collected some training expenses that more than cover your maintenance and upkeep of this money pit, not to mention the trainer's commission is mounting (he has no expenses, so it's all gravy to him) when you get the call about the "extra race on the overnite."

Now for those who are still learning, let me explain how this works.

Most races are part of a condition book that is basically a guideline of 20-30 days worth of racing, the conditions of the races, and when they will run. Every couple of days the racing secretary will add an "extra race" on the overnite, as a lure to get horses to enter. In most cases, these are races that powerful trainers and owners request to be written as they will have a horse ready for that particular day, distance, and condition. The racing office now needs to call around looking for five or six potential runner-ups for the race to actually have a chance to be written into the racing program. When your trainer gets the call, with the reminder of how many favors they can do for him, they will ask for your poor horse to be one of five or six sacrificial lambs in the proposed race. Your trainer has little choice but to agree. If he is that low on the totem pole where the racing office would feel comfortable to make the call in the first place, he will be in no position to refuse. So how does he call the owner to explain why the horse will be entered on such quick turnaround time? Well, he is not going to tell the owner that the racing office made him quiver like an inside curveball that broke late. He is going to tell you excuse # 89.

# EXCUSE 90
## "NEEDS A NEW ENVIRONMENT"

    Horses that need a new environment as per the handlers are usually horses that have a debilitating injury that they don't want the owner to know about. They would prefer that the injury fully bear its head in someone else's barn, thus passing on the blame. It will have nothing to do with the weather, surroundings, karma, track, or any of the other issues. They would want you to believe that a new place of residence would allow you to make the decision to move the horse elsewhere. Out of sight, out of mind would be a good description of the thought process here.
    That game that you played with the Hot Potato as a small child is what this part of the game is most like.
    Although, I must confess that lots of trainers start talking about horses needing a new environment when the winter comes around in the northeast. Next thing you know, the horse and the trainer have gone to a new environment and a warmer climate. Oh, and all this change, this is at your expense! Another paid vacation.

# EXCUSE 91
## "NEEDS A BUG RIDER"

Well, "weight can stop a freight train" is a folklore-like saying down at the track. It must be true since all those handicap races are for big money, and they lure mediocre horses to run against the best horses by assigning lesser weight on the mediocre horse. This is how the racing secretary tries to even out the competition in many a handicap race.

A bug boy is basically track and trainer speak for an apprentice jockey that gets a weight allowance in return for inexperience.

So you lose a race with a well-known rider who comes off the horse as if he did you a favor to ride him in the first place, only to be told that the horse was green, tired, short, breathing funny, jumping shadows, or any of the other excuses previously outlined. Well, next time you enter this horse, your trainer will tell you about the bug boy that has been getting on your horse every morning and how he thinks that taking the weight off can help win the race. He also tells you that the bug ruder will at least be hungry for a win.

My experience with this logic is that one of three things is really going on. The first scenario gives the trainer the benefit of the doubt, and he really does believe this theory. The second scenario is that the trainer doesn't think much of riders regardless of their experience, and the bug boy's agent has offered to split the commission with the trainer. Third and most likely is that your horse has real problems, and only the bug boy will ride him hard enough to win, risking life and limb (and your horse) just to win a race.

# EXCUSE 92
## "NEEDS AN EXPERIENCED RIDER"

When the second scenario as described in excuse # 91 occurs, but the horse ends up losing because the bug boy was in trouble the whole trip, the trainer loses his commission part of the purse. That is when you will be told that you need a rider with more experience. In my opinion, weight may stop a freight train, but experience and integrity should dictate the choice of rider.

# EXCUSE 93
## "NEEDS A RIDER WITH A BETTER LEFT HAND"

No, I am not kidding, this is really something I have heard. Read on to excuse # 94 to really chuckle!

# EXCUSE 94
## "NEEDS A RIDER WITH A BETTER RIGHT HAND"

Let me explain... Like baseball players and boxers, riders are professional athletes. Their skill is as astounding as it is dangerous, and they must be in phenomenal physical and mental shape in order to perform at the highest level. These athletes have to control the biggest, strongest, and fastest animals in the world, all from sitting in a saddle with all of the control in their hands and legs. Like other athletes, some riders are born lefty and some are born right-handed. No different than a southpaw or a right-handed hitter in baseball. There are both advantages and disadvantages in being either.

Some riders have a tremendous left hand stick, and some can crack a horse's rear hardest from the right side. Ultimately your trainer will let you know that you needed the other type of rider to have won today.

# EXCUSE 95
## "NEEDS A BETTER HANDED RIDER"

As we mentioned, riders with soft hands and a clock in their heads will almost always be the best rider for you if your goal is the winner's circle and coming out of the race with a sound animal. Occasionally even the best riders have bad days and, like a batter in a slump, will try too hard, sometimes pressing a little, which makes them seem a little out of character. Then there are the riders that just don't have a gentle hand and a clock in their head at all. When you get the good rider on a bad day or a bad rider on any day, you will be hearing sometime in your career of racing horses that the reason you lost is because the horse needs a rider with better hands.

# EXCUSE 96
## "STEPPED ON A STONE"

So your horse has another dull effort, and a dozen excuses have already been used in his short but economically draining career. You really want to pull your hair out and scream at the gods to ask why they are doing this to you as soon as you hang up the phone with your trainer.

He says they have good news. The horse has some type of abscess or foot bruise, and that's why he is not being the money-making machine that he should have been by now.

Foot bruise? How? you ask. Oh, it's nothing. He must have stepped on a stone in his last race or maybe even during training one morning. Don't worry, you are told, now that we know the problem it'll be no time before we get him back to the races and have some fun. You're happy and relieved as you feel vindicated that you and your horse had an excuse for that dull performance, never once wondering what a stone of that size was doing on the track. You just sit back and wait and wait and wait... Sixty days later, the bruise is healed and the abscess finally pops out so that the infection clears. Now you can at least go to the track in the morning and watch him get back to a training routine. That's got to be worth a couple of thousand a month, right? At least you're not losing!

# EXCUSE 97
## "STEPPED IN A HOLE"

Chipped knees, fractured cannon bones, splints, ankle problems, infected hocks, stifle problems, bad back, ulcers, and the myriad of other "stuff happens" ailments that happen on a racetrack are usually the result of bad training, poor conformation, or a combination of both. Throw in bad riding, bad feed program, etc., and there is no wonder why this is a tough business. However, when your horse comes back walking on two sides of the street at the same time—dead lame is one of the pet phrases used by the trainers—you can be sure that someone will suggest that the horse stepped in a hole. As if the track is a minefield, trainers will blame the surface as if 90 other horses a day have not run on it without incident!

## EXCUSE 98
### "CAN'T KEEP UP WITH THESE"

Blessed is the rider who comes off the horse with these kind words. It will save you tens of thousands of dollars! Be smart and heed this kind advice wrapped up in a bow!

# EXCUSE 99
## "NOT BRED TO RUN YOUNG"

Now, let me get this straight. Everyone went to the sale with Derby dreams and aspirations when buying this horse. We bought a horse that had mile and a quarter written all over his pedigree page. We started to breeze him early in his two-year-old year and have had him in the care and tutelage of a trainer for the last six months, and we are finally in a race. We finish dead last, as all the sprinters sprinted when we were still getting our sea legs out there. And now you tell me that the reason we lost is because the horse was not bred to win as a two-year-old. So I had only one question when I first heard this poor excuse of a reason. Why did you train him to race as a two-year-old? I guess he thought we'd get lucky!

# EXCUSE 100
## "NOT BRED TO BE HERE"

Trainer speak for "This horse is bred like a nanny goat, and even I would feel bad taking your money to train this one." Hallelujah, the truth shall finally set me free!